Effective Communication:

The Best Techniques

Richard Hawkins

Table of Contents

Additionally, the information in the following pages is intended only for informational purposes and should thus be thought of as universal. As befitting its nature, it is presented without assurance regarding its prolonged validity or interim quality. Trademarks that are mentioned are done without written consent and can in no way be considered an endorsement from the trademark holder.

Introduction

Congratulations on downloading *Effective Communication: The Best Techniques* and thank you for doing so.

The following chapters will discuss how effective communication is crucial for success in many areas of life and is an indispensable asset professionally. But this still involves much more than knowing what to say or being articulate. It takes in the use of verbal, non-verbal, as well as good written communication skills. Those who master this skill enjoy less stress because effective communication lessens friction and confrontation resulting from misunderstanding. Plus, it decreases the occurrence of mistakes due to poor communication.

Effective Communication: The Best Techniques looks at techniques to help improve communication as a whole by equipping you with ways to express ideas more clearly. While we will discuss verbal, non-verbal and written communications, we will also see how all these elements come together like paints on a painter's pallet, to convey a complete picture that includes, not only what you say, but how you say it, and what you mean. This includes what you "say" through non-verbal communication like facial expressions and body language.

Whether you own your own company, are a team leader, or run a non-profit, in order to be an effective communicator, you'll want to master all three forms of communication to help motivate the people under you. The techniques laid out in this book should help you do that with its practical advice and examples and even looks at how to develop open-mindedness, empathy and respect in your communication.

There are plenty of books on this subject on the market, thanks again for choosing this one! Every effort was made to ensure it is full of as much useful information as possible, please enjoy!

Chapter 1: The Role Communication Plays in Soft Skills and Techniques to Improve

To understand effective communication in relation to soft skills first let's define hard skills and draw the contrast between them and soft skills. Hard skills are specific, measurable skills that are learned. They generally require left brain logic and involve rules that stay the same no matter where you work. These skills are specific and can be defined in your cover letter when trying to sell yourself for a job or other opportunity. For instance, being proficient in Spanish, or earning a certain degree or certificate are considered hard skills.

Soft skills on the other hand are not quite so quantifiable because they are more concerned with interpersonal skills. These skills entail rules that change based on the company culture and expectations and are typically related to right brain thinking shaped in the emotional center. They include things like getting along with others, the customary code of behavior within your profession, and engaging in the give and take of small talk and listening. For instance, teamwork is considered a soft skill because it requires listening to others on the team and respecting the way they work even if it differs from the way you do things. This interpersonal aspect of teamwork is communication in practice. In fact, communication itself is considered a soft skill and is the first element needed for the rest of the soft skills desired in the workplace for both verbal and written skills.

Communication

While communication is considered a soft skill, it is also deemed vital because it is necessary for building relationships with those above or below you in the chain of responsibility. For instance, good communication can influence your performance for the better when you regularly engage in conversation with your manager, because through that interaction what she expects becomes clear. For your part, when it comes to a project, learn to clearly voice who, what, where, when, why, and how, and you'll become a valuable asset.

Set the Example: If your role is manager, invite a constant flow of communication from your team by setting the example. Greet people when you see them in the morning and set the tone for the day. Ask them questions, encourage them to share ideas and give them the freedom to express their feelings. Keep the door to your office open when possible, or just let your employees know they are welcome to knock on your door anytime. Taking steps like this builds a communication-friendly environment.

Cultivate Regular Significant Communication: Make significant communication a regular habit. Cultivate the habit. Don't wait for annual reviews to tell someone what they've done well or what areas need improvement. Instead, talk with people about how they are doing at least once a month. This not only lets them understand your perspective and what needs to change but it also opens the opportunity for them to tell you what they are thinking and experiencing.

Encourage Social Interaction: Also, foster an atmosphere of social interaction by encouraging employees to eat away from their desks during lunch hour. This gives people an opportunity to communicate and build relationships with their work colleagues as they share a meal away from the demands of their desk or work station.

Teamwork

Communication lays the foundation for successful teamwork, which brings about the solidarity necessary for a company's success. It creates a sense of unity as people fuse their diverse skills and work toward a shared goal. This in turn generates collaboration among co-workers which strengthens the quality of the work being accomplished. Overall, employers value team players because they help to foster a responsive, friendly work environment, which translates into satisfied employees and less turnover. Beyond that it also impacts the future as it creates an atmosphere that attracts new well-qualified talent.

Being a good team member means being able to clearly communicate your ideas with the group. You must be able to convey information via phone, email, and in person. Strive to always keep your tone professional but friendly. Both verbal and nonverbal communication are important when working with a group in person.

Generate Goodwill: How can you nurture teamwork in the workplace? Clearly communicate your ideas with the team with a friendly but professional tone. But both verbal and nonverbal communication are important, so practice being an active listener. Along with this, do what you can to generate genuine goodwill. When you have the opportunity, help a coworker when you see they need it. Offer to cover for them if they have a doctor's appointment, family emergency, or while on vacation. It's always nice to know someone has your back.

Adaptability

Today things constantly change creating new challenges, and so being flexible is important. When things don't go as planned, instead of getting angry or moody, or pointing the finger of blame at someone, it's important to adapt and work to find an alternative solution. Look at it as a new opportunity to let your creative side shine with the ability to adapt and re-assess. Just like communication lays the groundwork for teamwork, teamwork lays the groundwork for adaptability as the team learns to be flexible and to work together to find alternatives. Employers look for employees who are flexible and can adapt because they have the potential to be problem solvers, a valuable asset in any company. When faced with a difficulty an adaptable person:

- Accepts new challenges on short notice

- Has an open mind toward new strategies and ideas

- Improvises

- Keeps a positive attitude

- Persists

- Sees the bigger picture Stays calm

- Works with changing priorities

Be an Example: Challenge yourself to be ready to adopt change when needed. Consider getting training in the policy or procedure that needs to be revamped and propose teaching a workshop to pass on what you learn to your coworkers.

Problem-solving

Problem solving is an offshoot of adaptability and is an attractive soft skill employer's value. When things go wrong, instead of complaining or passing blame, problem solvers look for a way to resolve the challenge. Like adaptability, and teamwork, problem solving requires communication. It will not only get you noticed but it can elevate you to someone the company learns to depend on to circumnavigate unexpected challenges.

Think Before You React: To develop this skill, when a problem crops up, train yourself to think it through before reacting. Consider possible solutions and learn to approach your manager with a solution rather than a problem.

Critical Observation

Information itself doesn't mean much of anything if you don't know how to decipher it. In the case of this soft skill, instead of giving your manager a spreadsheet full of information, hand her a summary of that information with key issues highlighted, along with suggestions for possible next steps to take. This soft skill can be practiced and refined and brings a fresh perspective and innate solutions.

Learn from What You See and Use It: To become a critical observer, you need to be able to scrutinize data and put it to use. Beyond tables and spreadsheets, this also includes observing how people respond to information. Watch for patterns in behavior and reactions to information and what you learn can give you a better understanding of vital aspects of improving business operations.

Conflict Resolution

Conflict is an unwanted reality in the workplace. Some kinds of workplace conflict are quickly recognized, but other types might not be so easily spotted. Conflict can be something seemingly small but irritating like negative attitudes that eventually can lead people to be against each other. Oftentimes, conflict takes place at the senior level and requires some type of intervention, but really, anything that upsets or interrupts the office, affects production negatively, or presents a risk to other employees that needs to be addressed. How much a situation is tolerated before the conflict is addressed varies for a number of reasons. A manager might not feel intervention is needed for a minor exchange of words between employees, unless the problem grows into a daily incident or it expands beyond the initial employees involved. However, if one employee threatens another it should lead to immediate action.

Conflict Resolution Skills: Being able to constructively deal with conflict and work through disputes between people requires communication and demonstrates maturity. It requires a person who:

- Understands the problem: Someone who considers both sides of the issue.

- Acknowledges there is a problem: Acknowledging the concerns and frustrations is a big step toward resolving conflict.

- Is patient: Someone who takes the time to assess all the information.

- Avoids tactics like intimidation and bullying: Such tactics can make the problem stop for a time, but it isn't a long-term resolution and can actually make things worse.

Ignoring disagreements in the workplace is never the answer. Instead, they should be addressed directly but carefully. Those who take on the role of mediator, should allow both sides to express their complaints in an environment free of judgment where they can work together to find a solution.

Leadership

While you can take classes to help hone leadership skills, it really is a soft skill found in those who have an innate natural confidence and clear vision. Through communication and example, such people can help encourage co-workers and inspire them to get on board with management's ideas and new policies. However, leadership is really more about helping people reach their potential. Displaying leadership skills in this way can lead to new opportunities and may even lead to a raise or promotion. One way to step into a leadership role with future potential is to take an internship supervisor position. It not only provides the chance to manage people but will provide you with practical experience in learning how to motivate a team.

Leadership qualities to work on include the ability to:
Communicate: Leaders must be good communicators who can clearly explain specific assignments, jobs, goals, and other needed information to their employees. This includes giving employees valuable feedback in how they are doing without micromanaging. Overall, communication in a leadership role includes one-on-one conversations, departmental meetings, and conversations with the full staff, talking on the phone, and communicating via email. But here too, a big part of communication is listening. The flow of communication must go both ways between leaders and their team or staff so make sure are regularly available for discussions with employees.
Motivate: Leaders inspire their workers to go beyond what is expected. To do this, you must learn what works best to

motivate your team in order to encourage both desire and productivity. This can often be accomplished with rewards that encourage and build self-esteem, or by presenting employees with new responsibilities to grow their interest in the company.

Delegate: Leaders who take on too many things to be done will get bogged down and struggle to get anything accomplished. As a result, they aren't really leading. A strong leader learns to recognize the skillsets of his employees and then delegates by assigning responsibilities based on those skillsets. This frees up the time needed for other important tasks and all the work gets done.

Basically, you can be the best at what you do, but if your soft skills are lacking, you're actually limiting the odds of what you can achieve in your career. The Society for Human Resource Management did some research and found that employers that employers essentially have more interest in soft skills than technical abilities. That means soft skills are vital if you want to get ahead, and communication lies at the heart of it all.

Chapter 2: Techniques for Learning to Be an Active Listener

In the previous chapter, we established that being an active listener is an important part of effective communication, and it's a beneficial skill to employ in numerous kinds of situations from one-on-one interactions, to meetings and workshops, or even when addressing conflict. But what does it really mean to be "active" when it comes to listening?

The definition of the word *active* is to be "participating or engaged in a particular sphere or activity." In this case the activity is listening. It means a person is involved not just in hearing, but in paying attention to the words and learning to use them to draw out other important information that might otherwise go unshared from the other person or group. Like problem solving and critical observation, active listening is considered another interpersonal soft skill employers value because as a team leader or manager it is difficult to really identify what employees are thinking, what's bothering them, or how to help them unless you know how to listen to them.

When engaged in active listening, we must put our own thoughts (not to mention cell phones and other distractions) to the side and make a concerted effort to understand the other person's point of view. As we listen and learn how the person feels about the subject being discussed, we must practice tuning in to the underlying emotions and concerns reflected in their words. Remember, the purpose of active listening is to actually obtain more pertinent information. To accomplish this, it takes more than our ears. Body language involves our whole being and so along with listening ears making eye contact is also important. In fact, eye contact shows you are a good listener and it can actually build a connection and trust between you and the person talking. Also, as an active listener, your posture will reflect your interest with movements that show you are engaged like leaning slightly forward or sideways while seated. Other body language signals that denote active listening might consist of a slight tip of the head to the side or propping the head on one hand.

Along with the physical manifestations of being an active listener, there is a verbal aspect too. An active listener should ask short questions and make a comment here and there where needed. These verbal cues can help encourage the person talking to articulate their thoughts and reassures them that you're engaged – really listening, and that you believe what they have to say is important.

Active listening stands in clear contrast to how we normally listen during everyday conversation during which we often only give half of our attention to what's being said because we are more focused on what we want to say next. Active listening in the workplace means placing your focus on the person talking and, as you listen, asking for things like clarification or more details if needed but otherwise it is important to wait for them to finish. Listening in this way reflects:

- Interest

- A readiness to help problem solve

- A team player mentality

However, it is important to note that as you learn to be an active listener, not to fall into the snare of giving advice in a situation where counseling is the appropriate course of action.

Active Listening Techniques

This "active" component can be accomplished through a number of techniques which can build your listening skills including:

Building trust and establishing a bond: A good leader admits they don't have all the answers. As an active listener, they take time to listen to the ideas, feedback, and opinions of the people in their charge. As they listen, they don't interrupt, but stay in the moment other than to clarify what is being said. Then they use that knowledge to aid in the decisions and strategies they develop going forward. When you take the time to really listen in this way, it builds trust, a loyal devotion, and a commitment that establishes a bond.

Paraphrase what's being said to clarify communication: Often people *hear what they expect to hear* because of their own biases, expectations and stereotyping. When practicing active listening, paraphrasing is a tool that uses different words to reflect what has been said. When the person speaking stops talking and looks at the listener as if waiting for a response, the listener summarizes what they've heard using different words. This is a method of clarifying what they head. When doing so, it's important not to introduce your own biases or ideas and not to question the speaker's way of thinking, how they feel, or their actions. Resist the temptation to ask questions unless asking for clarification or for expanded details regarding what has already been shared. As we repeat the paraphrased version of what we heard, it offers the speaker the opportunity to correct any misunderstandings. Often this technique helps us see that we've misunderstood the speaker's intended meaning because we've ascribed our own meaning to what was said. This technique takes practice if we want the exchange to come across as a natural exchange. Before you start using it in the workplace, practice paraphrasing with people you know to avoid sounding forced or patronizing in a real-world situation. It does take a little work but learning a soft skill does come through practice and understanding and becomes a valuable asset on your resume.

Use of nonverbal cues to show you are listening: While active listening means giving the person speaking your full attention, it's just as important that the person speaking perceives that the listener is actively listening. We talked about the importance of body language as we listen, and the use of nonverbal cues is actually a technique used to convey interest it what the speaker has to say. This includes maintaining eye contact, leaning forward, nodding, smiling, and mirroring. Mirroring is the automatic copying of facial expressions used by the speaker. Such expressions denote sympathy and empathy in more emotional circumstances. However, mirroring is not forced but an automatic reflection, otherwise the listener can come across as disingenuous. Genuine visual cues can help the person speaking to relax. As a result, they are encouraged to communicate without difficulty in an open and honest manner.

Use of brief verbal affirmations: In the same way nonverbal cues show you are listening, brief verbal affirmation like, Yes," "Sure," "Mmm hmm," "I see," "I understand," "I know," or "Thank you," can be used to give the speaker the confidence they need to continue.

Ask open-ended questions: Open-ended questions have no fixed answer. There isn't a right or wrong answer and they don't tend to generate one-word responses close-ended questions. Instead, they encourage the person to steer the direction of the conversation with their answer which invites more open conversation because it gives them a sense that it's safe to express themselves and sets a collaborative feel to the conversation. These questions should be relative to the conversation in hopes they won't just help the person to identify problem areas but to also motivate them to make changes to correct the problem.

When asking questions, be sure to give the person enough time to answer and be careful not to ask a series of questions all at once or the person will start to feel like they are being interrogated. Remember, this is about active listening and the drawing out of information that normally wouldn't be shared.

Seek clarification by asking specific questions:
Clarification plays an important part in any communication and is a natural part of the active listening process too. In order to clarify as an active listener, the listener offers the essential meaning as they understood it, back to the speaker. This tactic ensures that the listener's perceptions and understanding are correct, or it offers the opportunity to resolve any confusion or misunderstanding.

Active listening is a soft skill that demonstrates both respect and understanding that can go both ways. If you find yourself in the situation where you are being asked the questions, active listening still lets you gain information and insight into the other person's viewpoint. It's not always smooth going, though, so remember that it doesn't profit you in any way to attack the person speaking or to put them down in any way. Instead, your role should be to:

- Be frank, open, and honest in your replies
- State your opinions with respect
- Deal with the other person by treating them the way you think they would want to be treated

Active listening reaches far beyond just staying quiet and giving someone your full attention. It entails being aware on multiple levels including things like body language, facial expressions, mood, and their natural interactive tendencies. While you're doing all this, you also need to be listening with your full attention. It's a lot of concentration to take in all at once, but with practice it offers a more complete picture.

Start utilizing active listening techniques today to become a better communicator. If you know you have poor listening habits (and many people do), it will take time to hone your listening skills. Old habits are not easy to break, but with practice, it can be done. Be purposeful in you listening. Remind yourself that your goal is to hear what the other person has to say. If you have trouble with this, mentally repeat what people are saying as they talk and gradually you will develop better listening skills. Also learn to ask questions, practice reflecting facial expressions and paraphrasing what you think was said. Practicing these techniques will help them become more natural when a situation dictates the need. And becoming a better communicator will improve your workplace productivity and help to develop better relationships.

Gather a group to practice active listening with exercises like the following on. It may actually be fun, but in truth you'll see what needs work.

- Break you group into two, As & Bs

- Have the B group wait outside the room

- Tell the A's that when the B's come into the room to listen to their partner, but every time their partner says something that makes them want to ask a question or think about something else they must raise their hand for five seconds and then lower it.

- Make it clear this is all they can do for the entire conversation. Other than that, they are not allowed to interact with Bs in any way but must stay silent. All they should do is lift their hand according to the preset rule.

- While the Bs are outside, they should be instructed to talk to As about something of interest that happened within the last six months when they come back into the room. It can be an experience, a hobby, their last birthday celebration – anything as long as it's positive. The have three minutes to tell their story.

- Have the Bs come back into the room, start the three-minute timer and tell them to "start talking."

- When the three minutes are up, ask those from the B group how they felt while talking to As. In general, they will probably mention things like not feeling listened to, or that they lost their train of thought because it was clear they weren't listening.

If you want, you can repeat it but allow the As to interact. This will paint a clear contrast between the two sessions. This is a fun exercise that doesn't take long. It is simple and doesn't require special materials. Following the exercise talk with the group about the potency of active listening. Discuss how they felt and what they learned.

Chapter 3: Techniques to Enhance Nonverbal Communication

People interact with one another at work all day long. As they do, they use both verbal and nonverbal communication, but what many people don't realize is that the way people deliver nonverbal messages can be just as important as what they say verbally. One commonly quoted statistic suggests that 93% of our daily communication is nonverbal. Nonverbal aspects of communication include gestures, eye contact, facial expressions, and even posture and general appearance. Other nonverbal communication involves aspects of speech like the tone of the voice, accent, how fast a person talks and things like that.

You've heard the old adage, "It's not what you say but how you say it," and that clearly applies when talking about the importance of nonverbal communication. For example, if someone says to you, "I appreciate how you willingly offer a helping hand when you see a need," and they say it while making eye contact, with a smile and amiable tone, you'll most likely consider it a compliment. However, if they say the same words using derisive inflections while rolling their eyes, scowling, and shaking their head, it's clear they are being sarcastic and critical. The verbal message is the same, but the nonverbal communication changed the meaning.

Elements of Nonverbal Communication

Eye Contact: It's a well-known fact that eye contact is an important aspect of communication. When you make regular eye contact you come across as more engaged, friendly, and confident, but the information generated by eye contact goes two ways because as much as it says you're friendly and confident, it also collects a lot of non-verbal information about what the person you're talking to is thinking and feeling. When you look away and avoid eye contact you miss that. A second benefit associated with making eye contact is that it compels you to mentally focus on the person you speaking with, which leaves you with less mental energy to think insecure thoughts.

When it comes to nonverbal communication, cues from the eyes are often subtle, but when we know how to "hear" what eyes are saying, we realize we can gain a lot of information from them. For instance, looking directly at the person you're speaking to shows your interest in them and helps communicate genuineness, candor and intensifies the sincerity of what you're saying. However, if you look at the person, but they don't look back at you, it's clear their attention is elsewhere. Even if they hear what you are saying, the lack of eye contact diminishes the personal connection between you and shows that you don't have their full attention.

If you're trying to make an effort to change someone's mind about something, the first action in the persuasion process should be to make eye contact. As you continue your conversation you want to sustain that contact with regular reconnections as you speak to them. However, you don't want to stare at them with prolonged or unblinking eye contact. That can be unsettling, because if you stare intently at someone without blinking, it can indicate aggression and can easily make that person feel uncomfortable.

When a person tends to look down or away a lot of the time while involved in a conversation, their nonverbal communication portrays a lack of confidence, or can be interpreted as a characteristic of submissiveness toward the other person. Also, it a person makes very little eye contact, it may indicate that they are lying. It has been suggested that our eyes indicate where the body wants to go. Liars often glance toward the nearest exit, "announcing" their eagerness to get away from the anxiety caused by lying. People who glance at the clock or their watches send the same message, announcing their desire to cut the conversation short. However, sometimes, liars who understand that not enough eye contact is a sign of lying, will overcompensate and purposely make eye contact longer than usual, but it tends to be unnatural and there are other nonverbal cues that indicate someone is lying, like throat clearing, jaw manipulation, hard swallowing, backward head movement or backward leaning.

Techniques to Help Improve Eye Contact

Throughout life, we all acquire little habits. Some habits are beneficial, but others can create challenges for us when we enter the workforce. For some people making too little eye contact is simply as a bad habit. For others, it may be that they are shy or socially anxious and making eye contact intimidates them. In most cases, the lack of eye contact is just a little habit that get in the way of solid teamwork and accountability. But like all bad habits, if you work on it, you can change. Here are a couple of techniques that can help.

Bridge of the nose trick: While looking someone in the eye is ideal, when you first start trying to purposely make eye contact, you may feel you are looking too long at someone. If that happens, train your eyes on the bridge of their nose between their eyes to take the stress off.
Practice with shorter conversations: When you aren't used to it, making eye contact for a shorter time rather than for a longer conversation is easier and a good place to start. Start to improve your eye contact skill by practicing during "throw away" conversations like with the cashier at the grocery store.
Practice as a listener: Making eye contact is easier when you are listening to someone rather than speaking to them. This is because listening allows you to focus on the other person without using mental energy to figure out what you're

going to say. This is the reason people don't usually make eye contact as much when they are talking. So work on making eye contact as a listener first, and then move on to incorporate it in a conversation.

Learning to make appropriate eye contact may push you out of your comfort zone, but developing this skill is worth the effort because it's been proven that our eyes communicate. As a result, failure to make good eye contact can actually put your ability get your ideas or to build personal or business relationships at risk.

Body Language: Research has confirmed that your posture – how you sit or stand – is a big part of how you come across to others. And your gestures combined with your posture accentuate the message you're sending. In fact, body language speaks louder that what you have to say verbally with a 55% impact on our communication. What you say makes only a 7% impact, and your tone, which will discuss in this chapter has 38% impact. So, when you mother used to say, "It's not what you say but how you say it," she was right.

Good posture communicates confidence: Whether you standing or sitting, good posture sends a message of confidence and makes people more willing to pay attention to what you have to say. An erect posture, while facing the other person directly, adds an element of assertiveness to your words, while slumped shoulders, a passive posture, or a tendency to lean back give the other person an advantage.

Gestures accentuate your message: Gestures strengthen your self-expression making what you say clearer. The key is to learn to accentuate your message using appropriate gestures that convey openness and warmth while adding emphasis. The relaxed uninhibited use of gestures can add depth to what you have to say, and even suggest openness and self-confidence. On the other hand, gestures you want to avoid include:

- Crossing your arms across your chest (signals defensiveness or a lack of openness)

- Pointing your index finger at anyone (comes across as threatening)

- Playing or fiddling with your clothing, jewelry, or pencils, etc. (shows you are distracted)

- Keeping hands in pockets or behind the back (gives a stiff or nervous appearance)

- Nail biting (demonstrates nervousness and insecurity)

- Finger tapping or drumming (reveals restlessness and impatience)

Facial expression: Your facial expression should agree with your message. Have you ever seen a parent trying to scold a toddler while trying to not laugh or smile? That's an example of a mixed message, and something you don't want to do professionally. But since facial expressions are closely linked to our emotions, they are many times involuntary and unconscious. For instance, if you manager lets you know that there's a new deadline that will require you work the weekend, a pensive scowl may creep across your face, or you may initially roll your eyes at the news. A better message to send might be to nod your head while making eye contact to convey a positive collaborative attitude. You want to make sure your expression sends the right message. One technique to help learn this skill is to practice making faces in the mirror. As you learn to control your facial expression, you can make it match what you are saying.

Body position: Where you stand when talking to someone also adds to your message. Granted, in the workplace you don't always have control over where you stand, but in general, when you stand side-by-side it may disengage you from the person you're talking to. Standing face to face may come across as confrontation, and so the best body position to adopt when possible is to sit or stand at an angle toward the person you're talking to. Additionally, if you sit or stand at the same eye level as the person you're speaking to, it indicates you are equal and diminishes any sense of intimidation.

Respect Personal Space: The distance from one person to another has a significant effect on communication. In general, the term "personal space" refers to the physical distance between two people in the same environment. In the workplace or among casual acquaintances, that space is generally between 3 feet to 10 feet. Respecting such boundaries in the office is important to maintaining professionalism. After you've worked with coworkers over time these lines can become blurred, but you must remember that others like supervisors may misunderstand if they see intimate gestures exchanged at work so keep your distance.

Using nonverbal cues is an important part of effective communication because it can enhance how people receive what you're saying. For managers, team leaders and others with managerial responsibilities this is an important skill to master, because their communication with employees directly influences their performance on the job. And since the manager's attitude is communicate more through nonverbal messages that what they have to say, these nonverbal cues can either cause positive or negative reactions and attitudes by employees and directly raise or lower morale.

Technique to Improve Nonverbal Communication

To improve your nonverbal communication, try to use some of these body language skills each day. The old adage, "practice makes perfect" hold true in this case because with practice, your nonverbal communication, and its influence on your communication overall, will become more persuasive, interesting, and effective.

Chapter 4: Techniques to Improve Topmost Verbal Communication Skills

Good verbal communications skills are essential for almost any job and as we learned in the previous chapters, effective verbal communication skills include more than just talking because how you deliver your message can often be more important that what you are saying. For this reason, people with good interpersonal skills who can deliver information clearly and effectively are highly valued in the workplace. They can make the difference between a team member and a team leader. In fact, when you're looking for a job, even if you aren't the most experienced candidate, good interpersonal skills can enhance your resume and give you an edge over the competition.

Among these skills, we covered verbal communication, nonverbal communication, and active listening in the previous chapters. Here we'll look at the remainder of the top interpersonal communication skills along with techniques for how to improve them. While we address them individually, they are all interconnected and work together.

Negotiation

Negotiation is a process that uses verbal skills to settle differences as both sides work toward resolution. This is accomplished through compromise or agreement with a goal to reach the solution while avoiding arguments and disputes. Good interpersonal skills are vital for successful negotiations, whether in formal or one-to-one situations. It requires not only knowing when to speak and what to say, but knowing when to be silent, because both sides intend to reach the best possible outcome for their organization. However, principles of fairmindedness, seeking mutual benefit, and preserving a relationship play key roles, and while these principles remain the same, there are different styles of negotiators with varying approaches to get the job done. But no matter the approach, as negotiators, they all need the interpersonal skills essential for effective communication to be successful.

Different Types of Negotiators

- Competitive negotiators: These results-driven competitive personalities are strategic thinkers. Their communication approach is focused, assertive and often even aggressive.

- Collaborative negotiators: These negotiators find creative solutions to satisfy both sides with an open honest style that takes the concerns and interests of the other party into consideration.

- Compromising negotiators: Compromising negotiators try to do what's fair for both parties as they seek to find a middle ground that can be agreed upon. They sooner compromise on your outcome to satisfy the other side.

- Amenable negotiators: These people use their negotiating skills to build and maintain relationships with the other party and tend to be highly responsive to emotions, relationships and body language within the negotiation experience.

- Avoiding negotiators: These avoiding personalities really don't make good negotiators. They often try to avoid situations that could result in conflict, and they might even try to stay behind the scenes because they find negotiations quite stressful and intimidating.

Best Techniques to Make You a Better Negotiator

Be prepared: Analyze and cultivate your best alternative to a negotiated alternative or agreement. Be clear on what you hope to get out of the arrangement because if you enter a negotiation without properly preparing, you're doomed to lose. Investigate the other side to know their strengths and weakness and to better understand what they want from the deal. Recruit the help of experts in the field as well as an accountant, attorney etc.

Consider timing: Timing is an important element in the negotiation process. Yes, you must be aware of what to ask for, but just as importantly you must perceive *when* you ask for it. It's a balancing act. At times it requires you to press ahead, but other times you have to wait. When things are looking best for your side, it's the time to press for what you want. But be cautious of pushing too hard because you don't want to destroy a long-term relationship in the process.

Check your ego at the door: As a negotiator it shouldn't be about who gets the credit for a successful agreement. Instead, a good negotiator works toward making the other side feel like the final solution was their idea.

Be an active listener: Resist the urge to think about what you're going to say next while your counterpart is talking. Instead, listen and learn from his arguments, then paraphrase what he said to be sure you have a clear understanding. Admit any problematic feelings behind the message, such as frustration. Using this tactic is likely to help you gain valuable information, plus the other side may mirror your example.

Expect compromise: Good negotiators expect to make concessions and anticipate what they might be. However, the other side is doing the same, so don't accept their first offer. Even if it's better than you'd expected. Politely decline and put on your best disappointed face. You never know what else you might get.

Demonstrate commitment to deliver: Commitment to deliver results on both sides keeps deals from unraveling. Avoid arrangements where the other side doesn't demonstrate commitment.

Problem Solving
At first glance the term "problem-solving" might seem straightforward enough, but to resolve workplace issues there are four distinct stages needed to resolve problems and it requires several important skills to, including strong verbal skills, to accomplish.

The four stages include:
- Defining the problem

- Brainstorming alternatives

- Choosing the best strategy

- Implementing your solution

Instead of going into detail regarding the four stages of problem solving, this chapter is going to focus on the problem-solving skills essential to work through those stages.

- **Observational skills:** During the early stages of problem solving, observational skills are needed to correctly evaluate what is going on and to identify the root cause of the problem. Instead of accepting issues based on how things look, the problem solver needs to exhibit lateral thinking and analytical abilities.

- **Innovative thinking:** As potential solutions to the issue are explored, the right approach won't come easily, and so the problem solver must demonstrate persistence. This process requires innovative thinking, in the second and third stages of problem-solving, where creative thinkers use their talent to think of approaches others overlook.

- **Balancing teamwork and leadership:** The fourth stage of problem solving, implementation, requires a skill set all its own. The problem solver needs to carefully balance teamwork and leadership as to prove their resilience to bear up to the unavoidable pushback from workers resistant to change. At this stage, negotiation and communication play an important role. And once the solution is implemented the problem solver needs to assess the results. This requires critical thinking and attention to detail to see what needs to be tweaked to be sure the problem is successfully resolved.

Techniques to Improve

When you improve your problem-solving skills, it gives you a clear-cut advantage in management roles as well as other positions. The following techniques can help hone your problem-solving skills by:

- Practice exercises like brain writing with a group. Participants write a few rough ideas for solving a particular problem on a piece of paper. Each piece of paper is passed to someone else. They read it silently and then add their own ideas to the page. The process repeats until everyone has added their ideas to each piece of paper. Gather all pages and discuss as a group what was learned. It can be things like: everyone in the group had a chance to have their ideas heard.

- Deal with everyday matters with a "what if" approach to regularly test new ideas
- Work logic puzzles and games like Sudoku

Decision Making
Decision making processes within a company are determined by things like leadership style and organizational philosophy. Some companies embrace a consensus-based approach, while others rely on management to make major decisions. It's also common for organizations to use a combination of centralized and consensus-based styles. So how an employee navigates and participates in the decision-making process within a company depends on their position within the structure of that company. So before applying for a position it's always important to research the company so you know how to highlight decision making skills on your resume and in your cover letter.

Overall, the critical skill in decision-making isn't really about learning a lot of techniques. It is more about knowing how and when to apply basic principles and the importance of continually reassessing and improving your methods.

Basic decision-making principles:
- Define the problem or opportunity

- Generate a variety of resolutions or responses

- Evaluate costs and benefits; pros and cons for each option

- Choose a resolution or response

- Implement the selected option

- Assess the result of the decision and adjust the course of action as needed.

Decision makers aren't always responsible for all six steps in this process but it is still a good idea for someone to go through all the steps in order to develop strategies to be sure nothing is overlooked and to be sure no biases had colored the original decision.

Techniques for Improvement
As we said, the decision-making skill isn't about learning a lot of different techniques, but these reminders can be applied to your skillset to help safeguard that you are making the best decisions.

- Examine your emotions and be sure they are not influencing your decisions.

- Don't base your decision on a single positive or negative aspect but look at it from multiple.

- When a decision is being made by a group, don't be afraid to ask for help from an objective outsider. Ask them to monitor the group discussions, challenge assumptions, and point to potential pitfalls.

- Create a group decision journal including expectations and the time-frame for evaluating results to make sure you don't fall victim to self-doubt.

- Keep a personal decision journal as well and include tips to yourself on how you will improve the process the next time.

Like all skills, developing decision making talents is an ongoing process. We learn from our mistakes as well as our successes and we learn from others who do it well.

Assertiveness

In some circles the term assertiveness has negative connotations, because people tend to mix it up with being aggressive. The Miriam-Webster dictionary defines assertive as "disposed to or characterized by bold or confident statements and behavior" such as an "assertive leader." So when considering interpersonal communication skills, assertiveness is a positive. It translates into the ability to express thoughts, feelings and beliefs in three ways: directly, honestly, and appropriately. That means that assertiveness, when correctly implemented, always respects the thoughts, feelings and beliefs of other people.

As an interpersonal communication skill, assertiveness relates to being able to express feelings, needs, and desires appropriately. The word appropriately is key to making this skill work for you. It means you can give your opinions and express how you feel, but when you disagree with something someone else says, you also have the ability to disagree respectfully. Like all these soft skills it takes practice for most of us to find the right balance.

This balance includes being open to express thoughts and feelings while also encouraging others to do the same, and it involves listening to other people's views and responding appropriately whether or not you agree with them. But beyond expressing thoughts and feelings and the ability to listen and respond appropriately, assertiveness also includes:

- Expressing appreciation for others

- Accepting responsibilities and being able to delegate

- Being able to admit mistakes and to apologize

- Exhibiting self-control

- Treating others as equals

Some people are more naturally prone to be successfully asserting themselves in this way. It's an inner attitude. But for those of us who aren't so naturally inclined, these techniques can help cultivate this skill and improve your ability to communicate in this way.

Techniques for Improvement
Before you can improve this skill, you have to identify which communication best describes you? Assertive, passive or aggressive. Once you've established this it will help you see what you have to work on. If you're style is passive, then you have to work on being more assertive and vice-versa. If you're lucky you'll be able to work on your naturally assertive style.

Exercise to become less passive and more assertive:
Focus on what you think, feel and prefer, because you have to identify these things in order to convey them to other people. Passive thinking might say, "It's not important," or "I don't know." If that's the way you're thinking it needs to stop.

- Practice verbalizing what you actually prefer. Start with things that seem unimportant to make it easier.

- Practice asking for things.

- Practice giving your opinion.

Exercise to become less aggressive and more assertive:

Start with little things. Consciously make an effort to let other people talk first. Work to stop yourself from interrupting others. If you do, catch yourself and apologize. Practice asking for other people's opinion and listen to what they have to say. If you disagree with what they say, try to express your thoughts without disparaging their viewpoint. Learn to soften your language. For example, instead of saying something is "stupid" say something like, "I don't care for it."

Techniques to build and expand assertive skills:

Even naturally assertive people can build and expand their skills. Take note of your current skills and identify your strengths and weakness to determine where you need the most improvement. Then look for a role model who represents an assertive style that's not too passive or too aggressive and emulate the qualities you think best. Practice in situations where you're comfortable and then challenge yourself to do the same in different situations.

Chapter 5: Techniques to Develop and Display Open-mindedness, Empathy and Respect in Communication

Many people reach a certain level of success in their careers due to excellent technical abilities or other attractive hard skills like earning a certificate or degree, but because their people skills are lacking it hampers their effectiveness because they don't get along well with other team members. Employees with poor people skills often find themselves at the center of unnecessary conflict which results in a stressful situation for everyone involved with negative consequences that can sidetrack the best-laid project plans.

When it comes to attaining hard skills, people are usually confident they can develop new skills through education, training, and experience. But when it comes to "soft" skills that deal with interacting with other people, they aren't so sure. People who say they aren't "a people person" often don't believe you can gain new skills to help in those areas because they embrace the idea that you just are what you are and there's nothing you can do about it, but that is not the case. For those who want to improve their soft skills, empathy is a great place to start to improve your people skills.

So where do you start? It boils down to communication again. You start by improving your verbal communication and related interpersonal skills. What does one have to do with the other? To be empathic, you need to be able to think beyond yourself and your concerns and to develop the ability to empathize with others. This takes communication, and as a bonus, once you start to understand others, they will start to understand you.

Techniques to Help Develop Empathy

- **Put aside your own point of view:** Work toward seeing things from the other person's viewpoint. As you start to do this more and more, it will become clearer that other people aren't being unreasonable, unkind or stubborn, but are most likely reacting to the information they have.

- **Acknowledge the other person's perspective:** Once you come to see what the other person thinks and why they believe what they do, acknowledge their perspective. People do have differences of opinion, and reasons to support their views. Acknowledgement of this doesn't mean you agree with them but is a step toward being better able to work together.

- **Take a closer look at your attitude:** A winning attitude does not mean getting your own way, being right, or even winning. If this is your attitude, then you don't have an open mind or an empathetic attitude. In fact, such an attitude shows you most likely won't have room for empathy in your life unless you change. Work toward a new priority – a change in thinking regarding what's important. Focus on things like finding a solution, building relationships and accepting others and it will help you change from the inside out.

- **Become a better listener:** Do you notice how this skill pops up repeatedly? Learning to listen is often more important than learning what to say. To become more empathetic, learn to listen to the complete message the other person is sending while using active listening techniques. Be sure to practice "listening" with your heart to hear what the other person is feeling too. When you're unclear about what they are saying, ask them to explain their position, and don't be afraid to ask them what they want. This not only shows you're listening but that you are interested and actually care.

Putting these skills into practice will give you the appearance of being more caring and approachable as you interact with people because your showing an interest in what other people think, feel, and experience. As your work on developing empathy, you can use this short checklist as a reminder of what to do, as you practice interacting with others through conversation:

- Notice physically and mentally what's happening

- Give them your full attention and listen carefully to what they are saying. Note the key words and phrases used.

- Respond receptively to the main theme of their message.

- Stay flexible. Be ready to change direction along with the other person's thoughts and feelings.

- Watch for cues that you're on target.

Developing Open-Mindedness
One of the reasons many people have poor people skills is because the isolate themselves from interaction. This tends to create close mindedness as people become set in their own viewpoint. Improving verbal communication skills can change this because communication allows you to connect

with others and build relationships and through them change your thinking, earn respect, acquire influence, and become more likable. Practice the following techniques to grow these skills and develop a more open mind:

- **Be approachable:** Communicate using a friendly tone and warm smile. This approach draws people to you because subconsciously it makes them feel good.

- **Think before you speak:** Often people think being blunt and speaking whatever is on their mind is a good thing. The problem is it ends up reflecting poorly on them. Learn to think before you speak because if you're not careful words you can destroy the very thing you're trying to build.

- **Be clear:** In today's world of tight schedules, people don't have the time or energy to figure out what someone is "trying" to say. Avoid being indirect or hinting at the point you are trying to make without saying what you really mean. Challenge yourself to speak directly making your message clear.

- **Avoid talking too much:** People tend to listen to those who carefully choose their words. On the other hand, people often lose their audience if they talk too much, and those who talk more than they should also run the risk of sharing information unnecessarily.

- **Be authentic:** You don't have to pretend to something you're not or put on a show to get people to listen to what you have to say. In fact, people are attracted to those who are transparent and speak from the heart.

- **Exercise humility:** Humility doesn't mean acting like a doormat, it's more about having a modest view of your own importance. This is considered one of the most attractive personality traits a person can have and is also a significant indicator that the person is respected. Those who show genuine humility and respect for others when they talk are held in high regard by most people.

- **Speak with confidence:** Confidence might seem like a contradiction to humility, but that isn't the case. You don't have to forfeit self-confidence to practice humility. Confidence arises from having an understanding of your true abilities, while humility is possessing a moderate opinion of your own importance. Speaking with confidence includes not only the words you choose to use but also the tone of your voice, eye contact, and other body language.

- **Pay attention to body language**: As we mentioned early, when we are engaged in face-to-face verbal communication, our body language can say more than our words. In this context, your goal is to use body language that communicates that you have an open mind as well as genuine respect and interest which will enhance the real meaning behind your words.

- **Be concise:** We already mentioned talking too much, but when a person doesn't get to the point of what they are trying to say it can frustrate and even irritate those who are listening. Plan ahead so you don't find yourself beating around the bush. Challenge yourself to find the fewest words to say what needs to be said while still being courteous and respectful.

- **Learn to listen:** Yes, being an attentive listener makes the list again because it's so vital in verbal communication – because communication goes both directions. It's important that you show a genuine interest in what is being said. Take the time to ask relevant questions, and work to listen for the message within the message.

How to Demonstrate Respect in the Workplace
Learning to demonstrate respect helps to avoid needless, insensitive, unmeant disrespect. Showing respect can be done in small ways that are simple and yet powerful in the way people perceive you. The following list is straightforward, and truthfully you probably won't find things you don't know, but you probably will find some that you don't put into practice. Make it your goal to show and encourage more respect in your workplace:

- Treat coworkers with courtesy, politeness, and kindness.

- Encourage others to voice their opinions and ideas.

- Before you express your point of view, listen to what others have to say.

- Don't speak over, interrupt, or cut off another person when they are speaking.

- Use other people's ideas to make changes or improve things at work. Be sure to let them know you used their idea or encourage them to implement the idea themselves.

- Avoid insulting anyone. No name calling, no putting down people or their ideas.

- Don't be a nitpicker. Constantly criticizing, belittling, or patronizing might seem trivial at the time, but it adds up and actually is a form of bullying. Needless to say, it doesn't cultivate respect.

- Pay attention to your body language, your tone when speaking, and your overall demeanor as you interact with others. Remember, many people "hear" what you're saying based on your nonverbal message.

- Make a conscious effort to improve your ability to interact with those around you at work. This means both bosses and coworkers. This will show them that you've grown more aware of the people around you and will open the opportunity to be more sympathetic.

- Be sure to treat everyone the same and implement policies and procedures in a consistent manner so people feel they are being treated both equally and fairly.

- Praise people much more often than you criticize. Also encourage employees to praise and recognize each other's accomplishments.

These ideas can help you lay a good foundation of respect. Once you consciously work at showing respect, you may be surprised to learn it is actually a cornerstone of meaningful work. Practicing respect won't just change you but will actually affect those around you to as you as the environment around you develops into a respectful, considerate, professional workplace. Improving your verbal and nonverbal communication skills requires intentional effort and an increased awareness and desire to improve. Your efforts to develop and display open-mindedness, empathy and respect in the ways you communicate will enhance your relationships, increase your self-esteem, and increase your value in the workplace.

Chapter 6: Best Communication Techniques When Making a Presentation

When a person is asked to make a presentation, most people picture someone standing at the head of a meeting room or auditorium with a microphone and a Power Point presentation. That can be an accurate image, but if we want to be an effective communicator we must remember that good communication is an exchange of information – even when giving a presentation. This exchange is shared in complex ways and will build on what we've already discussed regarding the basics of conducting a two-way conversation. But before we get into that aspect of making a presentation, let's discuss how to craft your presentation, including organization and structure.

Organize and Structure of Your Presentation

Words are powerful tools and should be thoughtfully chosen to convey the message you want to send when delivering your presentation. For this reason, it's important to really know your audience because words carry a literal meaning as well as invoke ideas and feelings. Such ideas and feelings differ from one culture to another and even from one business model to another. For instance, the word "dog" can invoke a happy or nostalgic feeling, but the word mongrel can draw out negative responses. So the first step in preparing your presentation is to choose your words carefully as you organize and structure the flow of your presentation.

To begin the organization process lay out all the content you want to include. Read this first draft and jot additional notes as they come to mind, and then read it again carefully. Watch for connections you hadn't thought of. See what fits with what, and as you do, various objectives and sections of the presentation will emerge.

Consider possibilities for a story to include as an essential component of your presentation. Depending on the content, it might even be an unconventional sort of story without characters, but its purpose will be to establish context around the content you plan to deliver. You want the story to include relevant backstory, with a before and after aspect that shows how the point you make fits the context of what is discussed in your presentation.

At the start of your story, ask a tactical question to prompt certain thoughts and ideas in your audience's mind. These can serve as jumping off points for your presentation. However, it's important that you actually incorporate the information you asked for in some way in your presentation to tie things together as a whole. Avoid using visual aids unless absolutely necessary but be sure to incorporate nonverbal cues to further communicate your point with the audience.

Don't be afraid to use uncomplicated and easy-to-understand objectives. Feel free to use things like: trends, opportunities, advantages, or something similar. Audiences appreciate a clearly-established flow that's easy to follow with upfront organization. Another plus with this approach is that it's easier for your audience to be engaged because they know what's coming next and don't have to spend their energy and concertation trying to figure out where you are heading.

Conclude your presentation by coming full circle – end where you began. Doing this reinforces what's been discussed and provides the perfect opportunity to remind your audience of the key points you've made. This is also a good place to make a reference back to the story you told to bring home the takeaway.

How to Craft a Memorable Presentation

Now that we've discussed organization, let's talk about ways to communicate that will make your presentation memorable. For this, think of your presentation like a piece of marble, and your words like a chisel working to craft the message into a work that clear and memorable.

Clarity: The definition of clarity is "clearness or lucidity as to perception or understanding; freedom from indistinctness or ambiguity." This explains what is to be expected in a presentation. When organized and structured correctly there should be only one way our information can be received. So be sure to select concrete, recognizable words that apply to tangible objects. These types of words are more likely to hold your audience's interest and be less likely to be misunderstood. In the effort to bring clarity to your presentation, avoid using more words than needed to express an idea – be concise.

Use vivid language: Again, if you imagine your presentation as a work of art, you want it to create an image in the mind of those listening to you because imagery is memorable. Use descriptive language including details like colors, sizes, and shapes along with strong verbs that work together to create mental images of objects, actions, or ideas. It's also important to write in an active voice, because using active voice for most of your sentences keeps them from becoming too wordy or complicated.

Rhythm: Your words and their arrangement create a pattern of sound. Other tools that help establish rhythm include: repetition, alliteration, and even the use of onomatopoeia for rhetorical effect. However, you don't want to overuse these language tools or it may cause the attention of the audience to lose focus on the point of your presentation.

The Role of Nonverbal Skills

Nonverbal signals can increase trust, clarity, and add interest to your presentation when delivered properly. In fact, it's worth your time to learn to become more sensitive to body language and nonverbal cues because it can make you a more effective presenter. Most people don't even give nonverbal cues a thought when they prepare their presentation, but if you aren't careful, your nonverbal cues can sabotage your presentation and convey an unintended message to your audience.

For instance, you may think you're being open, but if you turn your back or cross your arms you are sending them a different message because you're creating a barrier. And research shows that when people have a choice to believe visual cues or spoken words, most of the time they trust the nonverbal message.

Edward G. Wertheim, author of *The Importance of Effective Communication*, defines five main results nonverbal communication can have (good and bad):

- Repetition: Nonverbal cues can emphasize what is already being said

- Contradiction: They can contradict the message and make the speaker seem untruthful

- Substitution: They can take the place of words

- Complementing: They can complement a verbal message

- Accenting: They can emphasize a certain point in the presentation

So as you prepare to deliver your message, go over the following checklist to have it fresh in your mind, to avoid sending the wrong message:

Checklist for Good Nonverbal Cues

- Dress to suit your audience, but as a presenter, dress a little more formally than usual.

- Exhibit energy and enthusiasm

- Make appropriate eye contact

- Maintain good posture

- Engage in purposeful movement

- Use natural gestures

Connecting with Your Audience

Before your presentations begins, take time to introduce yourself as people come in. Engage them in light conversation and get them to talk about themselves and why they are attending. Once you're ready to start, remember that audiences don't want to be talked at. They aren't looking to sit in one place for an extended amount of time while content is dumped for them to absorb. Instead, most audiences prefer a delivery of information that combines a certain degree of formality with the best characteristics of good conversation. They want it to be direct, but spontaneous and animated. So with that in mind, look people in the eye one at a time once you start talking. Hold their gaze for 5 seconds or so, and then make eye contact with someone else. If it's a larger audience, don't neglect people at the back or up in the balcony. Look at them too and make it clear that you know they are there – that you care. This will help them stay engaged, even when you are interacting with those sitting in seats closer to the front. Also use vocal and facial expressions to energize things as you give your presentation.

Do your best to keep your delivery fluid as you communicate what you've prepared. Don't sound like you're giving a speech, and absolutely don't read your presentation unless you want to put people to sleep. The cadence of your voice needs to be natural, and if you follow the cues offered by your audience, it will make you a better speaker as you adapt to their feedback, verbal and nonverbal.

If it's clear a listener is bored or confused, you'll want to adapt your verbal and nonverbal message – this can be done in a number of ways. You might try injecting a little humor or taking a moment to explain more regarding what your listener found confusing, and sometimes, you might even choose to change the course of your presentation as long as you know the topic well enough to pull that off. If you're willing to be flexible, you have a better chance to get our point across while keeping the audience engaged. If, instead, you stick to a rigid communication style, you will most likely lose that spark between yourself and the audience.

Audiences have a limited attention span. To become a more effective communicator, think about making your presentation interactive. Ask the audience a question, encourage people to call out their thoughts during a brainstorming session or at least ask hypothetical questions to engage the audience. Another way to involve the audience is to give them a preview of the topics that will be discussed. This outline is a valuable way to get audiences excited about the presentation and helps them to focus on your message and on key takeaways.

Technique to Improve Your Presentation

Make arrangements to record your next presentation. Then listen to it and count how many times you used the word "I." Also pay attention to other times when your language could have been more focused on the audience. Work from the perspective that the people don't care about you but only care about themselves. When you approach talking to a group with this mindset, you can't go wrong! Instead of talking about what "I can offer," approach the audience in a way that tells them what they will gain. "In the next half hour, you will discover..." Even something like changing a single word can make an astounding difference in your presentation.

Communication can be summed up as the exchange of information. Given the complex ways that we receive and perceive messages, however, this exchange is far from simple and straightforward. To improve your communication skills, first work to master the basics of having a two-way conversation.

Conclusion

Thanks for making it through to the end of *Effective Communication: The Best Techniques*, let's hope it was informative and able to provide you with all of the tools you need to achieve your goals whatever they may be.

The next step is to follow the practical advice supplied in this book to help hone these valuable communication skills. Carry what you've learned about verbal and nonverbal communication into your workplace and put it into practice. Train yourself to read the body language of others to better understand what they are saying as well as what message you're conveying to others. Start utilizing active listening techniques to become a better communicator and practice paraphrasing what others have said to clarify what you think they mean. This gives them the opportunity to correct any misunderstandings and lets them know you are really interested in what they've said as well as what they mean. In the same vein, learn to use nonverbal cues like maintaining eye contact, leaning forward, nodding, smiling, and mirroring to show your interest in what others have to say.

In most cases, the lack of eye contact is just a little habit that gets in the way of solid teamwork and accountability. But like all bad habits, if you work on it, you can change. Whether you own your own company, are a team leader, or run a non-profit, in order to be an effective communicator, you'll want to master all these forms of communication to clearly communicate in order to help motivate and encourage the people under you. Follow the techniques laid out in this book and with practice, your nonverbal communication, and its influence on your communication overall, will become more persuasive, interesting, and effective.

Finally, if you found this book useful in any way, a review on Amazon is always appreciated!

CPSIA information can be obtained
at www.ICGtesting.com
Printed in the USA
LVHW082235180819
628092LV00015B/907/P

9 781720 453598